POSITIVE STEPS

Dealing with Bullying

by Susan Martineau

with illustrations by Hel James

Smart Apple Media

Published by Smart Apple Media
P.O. Box 3263, Mankato, Minnesota 56002

Printed in the United States of America at Corporate Graphics, in North Mankato,
Minnesota.

Library of Congress Cataloging-in-Publication Data
Martineau, Susan.
  Dealing with bullying / by Susan Martineau ; with illustrations by Hel James.
      p. cm. -- (Positive steps)
  Includes index.
  ISBN 978-1-59920-491-8 (library binding)
  1. Bullying--Juvenile literature. I. Title.
  BF637.B85M38 2012
  302.3--dc22

                                                          2010053877

Created by Appleseed Editions, Ltd.
Designed and illustrated by Hel James
Edited by Mary-Jane Wilkins
Picture research by Su Alexander

Picture credits
Shutterstock; 4t Mandy Godbehear/Shutterstock, b Monkey Business Images/
Shutterstock; 5 Cheryl Casey/Shutterstock; 7 Yuri Arcurs/Shutterstock; 8 Cheryl
Casey/Shutterstock, background 1000 Words/Shutterstock; 9 Emese/Shutterstock;
11t Andreas Gradin/Shutterstock, b Sonya Etchison/Shutterstock; 12 Monkey
Business Images/Shutterstock; 13 background AraBus/Shutterstock; 14-15 Thumb
/Shutterstock; 17 Gelpi/Shutterstock, background Vlue/Shutterstock; 1
8-19 background Diane Uhley/Shutterstock; 20 Mandy Godbehear/Shutterstock;
21 Andrey Shadrin/Shutterstock; 22-23 background Nigel Paul Monckton/
Shutterstock; 23 Monkey Business Images/Shutterstock; 24 Kalnenko/Shutterstock;
25 Ron Hilton/Shutterstock; 26 Sonya Etchison/Shutterstock; 27 Monkey Business
Images/Shutterstock; 28-29 Lakov Kalinin/Shutterstock; 32 Sonya Etchison/
Shutterstock
Cover: Shutterstock

DAD0048
3-2011

9 8 7 6 5 4 3 2 1

Contents

I'm fed up with bullies.

What Is Bullying?

If people do something or say something to try to **hurt** you, they are bullying you. Bullies keep doing it even when they know you are upset.

They're picking on me.

Leave that alone! It's mine!

They're always whispering behind my back.

4

I feel really left out.

She's always punching or hitting me.

These children are all being bullied. There are different sorts of bullying. Hitting or punching is bullying, but nasty words can be just as **hurtful**.

LET'S TALK ABOUT . . .

How do you think these children feel? Look at the words on the right. Can you think of any other words to say how you feel if you are bullied?

scared

upset

stupid

hurt

lonely

That's Not Funny

What's wrong with your hair, Laura?

Laura is fed up with being **teased** at school. She likes jokes, but not when they are always about her. She feels picked on.

You look like a boy.

Bullies use words like this to make fun of people. They like people to laugh at what they are saying. This makes them feel smart and **powerful**.

What can you do?

Standing up to a bully can be scary, but bullies need to be stopped. If you see that someone is unhappy about being teased all the time,

- Don't join in with the teasing.

- **Ignore** the bully. Bullies like people to listen to them.

- Be friendly to the person being teased.

The Name Game

This game makes everyone feel good. Write your names on a piece of paper. Everyone picks a name, without looking. Now write down three good things about that person. Take turns reading the names and all those good things out loud.

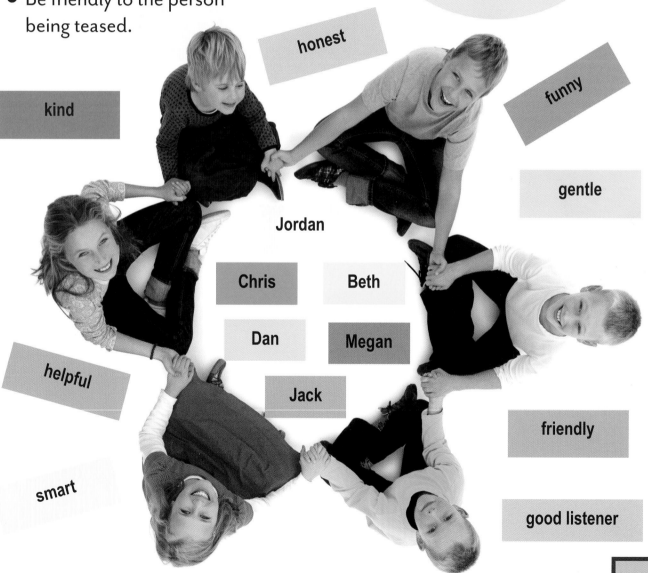

honest

funny

kind

gentle

Jordan

Chris   Beth

Dan   Megan

helpful

Jack

friendly

smart

good listener

They Scare Me

Sometimes bullies use words to frighten other people. They shout at them or **threaten** them. This can be really scary.

You can't play here. Go away!

If a bully is shouting at us like this, we can sometimes feel as if we really have done something wrong even though we have not.

Give me that or I'll hit you!

Why do you think some bullies threaten people by shouting at them? Is it to make themselves look big? Perhaps they are really feeling small inside.

What can you do?

If you are being bullied like this, it is very important to get help.

If you see someone else being yelled at, you should get help for them.

Try to talk to someone you **trust**. An older student or an adult will be able to help you.

Telling someone about the bullies is the first step toward dealing with them.

You're Hurting Me!

Some bullies hurt others by kicking, punching, hitting, or pinching them. Hurting others is always wrong.

What can you do?
Some people will tell you that if a bully hits you, you should hit back or run away. These things will not stop the bully, so the best thing to do is to ask for help from an adult you trust.

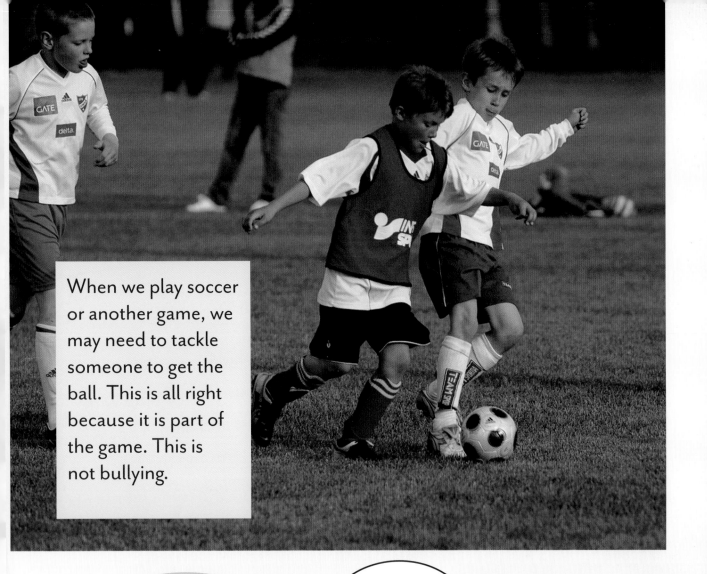

When we play soccer or another game, we may need to tackle someone to get the ball. This is all right because it is part of the game. This is not bullying.

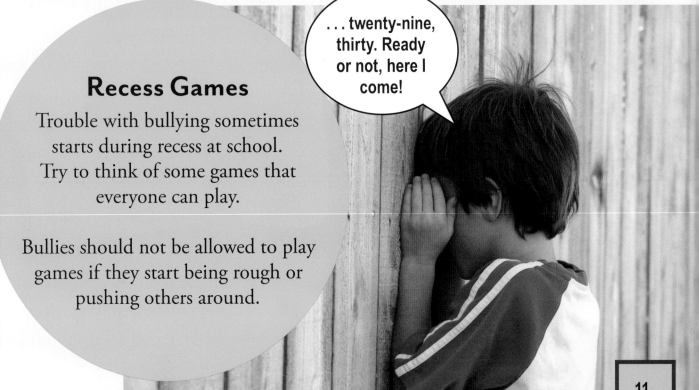

Recess Games

Trouble with bullying sometimes starts during recess at school. Try to think of some games that everyone can play.

Bullies should not be allowed to play games if they start being rough or pushing others around.

They Don't Talk to Me

Sarah feels lonely and sad because some girls in her class keep whispering about her. They never let her join in any of their games. She's writing to her dad who is away from home.

Dear Dad,

I'm glad it's nearly summer because I am fed up with Cassie and Sam. They whisper about me and think I can't hear them. They won't let me play with the other girls either. It makes me feel really left out.

I can't wait to see you.

Love,

Sarah xoxo

When someone like Sarah is always left out and ignored, she is being bullied.

What can you do?

There are several ways to help someone like Sarah:

- Talk to her and be friendly.

- Ask if she would like to play with you.

- Don't join in with girls like Cassie and Sam.

What's your favorite game?

Making Friends

Go up to someone you have not played with before. Ask them about themselves and see if they would like to play a game with you.

Do you have any brothers or sisters?

When's your birthday?

He Took My Best Friend

Bullies like to boss other people around and tell them what to do. A bully might sometimes try to take away our friends. Ryan and Jordan were best friends until Tom came along.

Bullies often seem to have lots of friends, but they are not very good at **sharing** them. Their friends may be too scared to play with anyone else.

Jordan was my best friend.

Now he always does what Tom wants.

LET'S TALK ABOUT . . .

Look at these words. Choose the ones that tell you how Ryan is feeling. Now pick the ones that might be about Tom the bully.

ignored

sad

selfish

bossy

left out

hurt

What can you do?

Learning how to share friends is very important. Here are some ways to keep your friends happy:

- Try not to leave anyone out of games or jokes.

- Listen to what they are saying.

- Don't be bossy!

Don't Tell, or Else!

Paul is writing to his friend from his old school. He is having some trouble with bullies.

Hi Arjun,

It's OK at my new school, but last week I saw some boys doing something really bad. They broke a window and they keep telling me not to tattle. They won't leave me alone.

I'm not looking forward to school on Monday.

See you soon,

Paul

*Sometimes bullies try to get us to **lie** for them or keep quiet about something bad. What do you think Paul should do?*

What can you do?

Paul needs to tell someone the **truth** even though it is a bit scary. The best people to talk to are his parents, a teacher, or another adult that he trusts.

If Arjun was there, then he could go with him, but perhaps Paul has a friend at the new school who could help and **support** him.

Come on, I'll go with you.

That's Mine!

Some bullies are always taking other people's stuff or breaking things that do not belong to them.

Bullies do not understand about sharing and **borrowing**. They have no **respect** for other people's belongings. They do not care how we feel when they keep taking our things.

It's mine, not yours!

Give that back!

LET'S TALK ABOUT . . .

Imagine what would happen if everyone just grabbed what they wanted or smashed other people's things. Learning to share and borrow from each other is really important.

What can you do?

- If you want to borrow something, you need to ask first.

- If someone asks to borrow something of yours, then it is helpful and kind to say yes.

- Think of the phrases you might use.

- Don't forget to give things you borrow back!

Who Are the Bullies?

Bullies come in all shapes and sizes. They can be boys or girls. Sometimes bullies walk around in groups or **gangs**. Bullies pick on other people for many different reasons.

They're not very sure of themselves.

Maybe they are unhappy at home.

Some bullies have been bullied themselves.

They're spoiled and think they can do and say what they like.

LET'S TALK ABOUT . . .

Do you agree with these children? Are there any other reasons why someone might start being a bully?

Bullying and hurting people makes bullies feel powerful.

What can you do?

If you think you may be a bully, you need to try to think about why you are doing it. Try to imagine how the **victim** is feeling.

If you are being bullied, do not be afraid to ask for help from someone you trust. It could be your parents, an older student, or your teacher.

I Didn't Mean to Be a Bully

Ellie is in a group of friends who all stick together at recess. They've been picking on some of the other girls.

Hi Ally,

Sorry I haven't written for a while. I've been in trouble at school. I feel really bad because I didn't mean to hurt anyone—we were just having fun. We all said sorry and promised not to do it again, so I think it's OK now.

See you soon,

Love Ellie

LET'S TALK ABOUT . . .

Having a group of friends is good, but sometimes a group can start to bully other people. One person might make a mean joke about someone else to make everyone laugh. They might not even mean to be hurtful, but it can feel like bullying when everyone else joins in.

I don't think that's funny.

What can you do?

It can be hard to stand up for what is right, but:

- Don't get caught up in bullying.

- Tell the others in your group that it is not right.

- **Apologize** to the person you have hurt.

- Try to think about how the bullied person feels.

23

How Can I Help?

If our friends are being bullied or we see anyone else being bullied, we need to know what to do. We should not just walk away or ignore the bullying.

When someone is being bullied, they need extra friends. Bullies find it harder to pick on someone who has a friend to help them.

You can't play because you're no good at sports.

Yeah, you're really bad.

If you watch someone being bullied and do nothing, you are almost as bad as the bully yourself. Can you be brave enough to help? How would you feel if someone didn't help you?

What can you do?

- Tell the bully or bullies they are wrong.

- Don't leave the bullied person on their own.

- Help everyone in trouble and not just your friends.

- Get a grown-up or someone older to help.

- Don't ignore the bullying or just walk away.

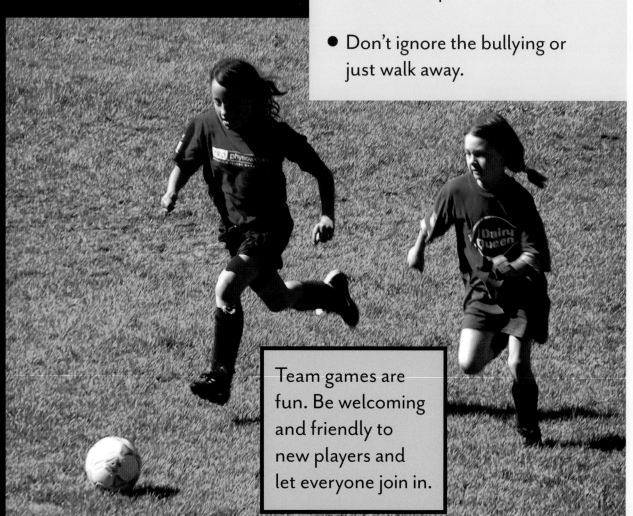

Team games are fun. Be welcoming and friendly to new players and let everyone join in.

What to Do if You Are Being Bullied

If you are being bullied, you might feel scared and alone, but there are lots of people who will want to help. Remember that it is not your fault that you are being bullied. There is nothing wrong with you. It is the bully who is wrong.

David is bigger than me and he told me not to show the bullies I was upset.

He talked to them, and I think they've stopped because they can see he is looking out for me.

What can you do?
Do not keep things to yourself because you think you are being a tattletale if you ask for help. That is what the bully wants you to think. You need to be brave, but it will be worth it.

Think of the person you trust the most and talk to them. It might be a friend, someone older than you, your brother or sister, your teacher, or your mom or dad. They will want to help. You will not be alone.

Making the Right Choice

We need to understand bullying so that we can deal with it. We want to be able to help others who are bullied or get help if we are being bullied. We also need to make sure we are not being bullies ourselves.

What can you do?

Find the bold words in the book. Check that you know what they mean by turning to the glossary on pages 30–31. Try making your own sentences using these words.

Use the sentences to start your own list of ways you can deal with bullying.

All the bold words are explained on pages 30–31.

What can you do?

Talk to someone you trust.
Don't say hurtful things.
Share your friends.

Get help and don't just put up with bullying.

Say sorry if you hurt someone.

Glossary

apologize
to say you are sorry for something you have said or done

borrow
to use something that belongs to someone else and agree to give it back

gang
a group of people who do things together

hurt
to upset someone or to make them feel pain

hurtful
something that hurts us or our feelings

ignore
to take no notice of someone or not to listen to them

lie
to say something that you know is not true or that you do not believe

powerful
very strong

respect
to show you care about other people's feelings and belongings

share
to let other people use your things or become friends with your friends

support
to help and encourage someone

tease
to make fun of someone

threaten
to say you will do something bad if someone does not do as you say

trust
to believe that someone is good and honest and will want to help you

truth
what is true or what really happened

victim
someone who is being hurt

Web Sites

It's My Life – PBS Kids: Beat the Bully
http://pbskids.org/itsmylife/games/bullies_flash.html

Kid's Health: How Cliques Make Kids Feel Left Out
http://kidshealth.org/kid/feeling/school/clique.html#

Pacer Center's Kids Against Bullying
http://www.pacerkidsagainstbullying.org/

Index